Emotional Intelligence through NLP

Boost your Self Esteem, Happiness, and Confidence through Neuro-linguistic Programming Declutter your Mind, Kill Negativity, and Create Positive Thinking for a Successful Life

Ben Partell

1

Table of Contents

Introduction

Congratulations on purchasing *Emotional Intelligence through NLP to create a happier and more successful life.*

The following chapters will discuss various techniques of NLP to help you change your mindset to live a happier and more positive future. We will start with what NLP is and end up with NLP techniques you can use to change your life.

There could be many reasons why you have found yourself here today. Maybe you have been feeling very negative lately, and you're tired of feeling down. This is something a lot of people suffer from, so don't think that there is anything wrong with you. Negativity happens, but it's how you respond to it that can change your outlook on life. If you allow one single bad thing to send you into a spiral of negativity, then everything in your life will seem unbearable. But with the right tools, you can find the positive in any negative situation and instead of running away from your problems you can and accept them and move on.

You could also be here because you are tired of struggling with phobias and fears. A lot of people have fears or phobias. Some don't have much of an impact on their life, while others impact their life greatly. If you find yourself having a hard time leaving the house because you are afraid that you will face your fear or phobia, then you definitely need to work to overcome it. This has a major negative impact on a person's quality of life. You don't get to experience new things or do things that you have always loved doing. Instead, you are constantly worrying about avoiding the things you are afraid of. The good thing is that this book will help you to overcome those fears that hold you back so that they don't rule your life.

Ultimately, everybody is here to gain a positive mindset. The world can be a struggle. Bad things seem to happen every day, so it's easy to get caught up in the negativity. But this book is here to help you out of the funk and find happiness in everything.

Whenever you get caught in positivity or negativity, you will continue to get more of the same. That means if you are always complaining, things didn't go the way you wanted, or you simply hate Mondays, all you are going to get in life are negative thoughts and beliefs surrounding those thoughts. You are going to continue feeling bad and lousy, and it won't look like there is a way out of all of this negativity. The opposite is true, as well. If you see the good in things, are happy for the things you do have, and rejoice every day you wake up, then your life is going to be happier.

Your outlook in life doesn't just affect you, but it can affect the people around you as well. Negativity is a tricky thing. What you may see as negative may not be negative to another person. But, in general, negativity will cause the energy surrounding you or things to feel harmful, unhelpful, and dense. Some of the most common forms of negativity that people can agree on are aggression, self-pity, jealousy, impatience, low self-esteem, and gossiping.

Constantly filling your life with negativity can affect your future. What you think you will form your future. So if you are in a negative state, you will create a future of more of the same. This is why it's important to conquer a negative mindset with positivity because we can easily create vicious cycles in life, when thinking negatively, which make them extremely hard to break. This can then prevent you from living up to your full potential.

Negativity can also harm others. You could end up projecting those negative thoughts on others, be in a bad mood, or use negative words. This reinforces your negativity and makes other people feel bad, as well.

This low vibration energy can also impact your physical body. When you experience negative emotions, eventually, it is going to reach your physical body, and we all know what stress can do to you.

That said, this book isn't trying to tell you to be positive all the time because that's impossible. Instead, this book is about accepting negativity instead of running away from it, finding the good in things and shifting your mindset to a point where your subconcios thoughts are positive and positive outlooks on situations are what you see first rather than the negatives. Positivity can help you get through the rough times in life. When you are feeling down, you can list out some things you are grateful for, and it can lift your mood.

You and everybody else have to accept your negative emotions to help you work through them. You can't reject yours, and you can't make others reject their negative emotions by simply spewing positive affirmations. That's why I want to make sure you don't cross the line into toxic positivity because it is really easy to do when you are trying so desperately to make your life happier.

Here's an example of weak positivity; "Think happy thoughts!" That sounds good in theory, but when a person is feeling down, that's the last thing they want to hear, and it likely isn't going to live them up. Instead, saying something like, "It's probably hard to be positive at the moment, but I'm sending out some good energy to help you through this," can be more helpful. This holds true for the way you treat yourself, as well. More people fail at being more positive and happier because they think they can't think of a single positive thing. Acknowledge the tough times and work through them to the happy, and NLP will help you do that.

When it comes to dealing with yourself, make sure you greet that negative emotion with compassion. Recognize that it's tough and accept the fact you feel that way. This instantly takes the power away from the negativity. This is just another part of being human. You can't make yourself feel happy, 24/7.

When was the last time you read a self-help book that seemed straightforward with information that you understood what to do with? You may have ahd a few, but by and far, most drone on and on about problems and things you should avoid, but very few give you clear steps as to what to do to improve your life. That's not what you're going to find moving forward.

You're here to make a change, not to get frustrated. Frustration is a negative emotion, and we've already talk about how how negativity can affect you. I want to bring you positivity and healing, and that's exactly what you'll get.

Through the use of NLP, you can learn how to find the right amount of positivity so that you can live in the now and not in the clouds. With the information inside, you will learn what NLP is along with techniques that you can use to improve various areas of your life. We won't bore you to death with a bunch of information. You will find actual step-by-step techniques that you can start using right.

One last thing before we continue, this can take some time. Nothing happens overnight. Some may see changes as soon as they start practicing NLP, but others will have to practice several times before changes are noticeable. Don't stop using these practices. The more you do it, the the better you will get at it and the more it will help you. With time, you will notice changes in your life.

Chapter 1: What is NLP

NLP, neuro-linguistic programming, is a skill set that reveals the type of communication that is most important. To help you understand NLP, let's break down the name into three sections.

Neuro – This refers to the brain or mind, especially in regards to how the state of the mind and body affect actions and communication. NLP will provide you with a structural way of viewing the body and mind states, creating mental maps that show the way things happen, and how you can change your mindset.

Linguistic – This refers to the fact that the body and mind states are revealed through the things that are said and our non-verbal language. Language is how we gain access to how the mind works. The language patterns of NLP show us how to get a hold of unconscious information that otherwise would reaming unknowable and vague.

Programming – This is our capacity for changing the body and mind states. Ever heard of the saying, living on autopilot? To a trained NLP practitioner, this might mean that you are simply living by your programs, which are made up of habitual traditions, beliefs, reactions, feelings, and thoughts. A person trained in NLP knows how these programs work in the mind and how you can access them using language so that our autopilot actions are able to be changed.

How it Works in Real Life

For the most part, when we are having a conversation, we focus on the words. What are they saying and how should I respond? For a long time now, we have known that words have the least meaning in communication, conveying just seven percent.

If a person were to tell you that they are willing to help you put together a social get together, but they have a tone that is flat, and their face looks as if you invited them to leech letting ceremony, it's pretty obvious they aren't being honest. While they may be verbally saying yes, non-verbally, they are telling you the opposite.

NLP makes up the other 93% of communication. NLP gives you a way to understand and use communication that is important. When you master non-verbal communication, you will be a master of communication.

There is another interesting part of this. The majority of people don't actually realize that communication has more to it than simple interactions between individuals. There is an entire world of communication that lives in your body and mind. Your inner life, which is your feelings, mindset, and attitude, is also an active form of communication.

Inner communication is a big part of NLP, which used to be called the "study of the structure of subjective experience." This is basically a fancy way of saying that NLP can help you to figure out the things that are going on in your mind so that you are able to do something to help this process.

For example, let's say that friends are coming over, but you are feeling rather tense. You aren't quite sure why. On the surface, everything is fine, but you still feel like you are right on the edge. NLP practitioners are able to figure out how you are causing this tense state in your mind. It has to do with the way you are communicating with yourself.

History of NLP

While you have likely heard of Richard Bandler and Jon Grinder as the creators of this practice, NLP was actually created by several people who constantly made contributions. This group was made up of Grinder and Bandler along with David Gordon, Leslie Cameron, Judith Delozier, Robert Dilts, Frank Pucelik, and many others.

In the early 1970s at the Santa Cruz campus of the University of California, this group of people set out to find the communication patterns that provided psychotherapists, like

Fritz Perls, Virginia Satir, and Milton Erickson, to reach uncommon results. Through the use of videotape analyses and direct observation, they broke down the communication patterns of people and taught them to other people.

They used what is known as modeling to discover transformative communication. Most people consider modeling to be the main component of NLP. When you understand how to come up with a model based on how experts do things, you are able to teach and learn any new skill.

The first thing that they discovered was that Satir would make her adjectives, verbs, and adverbs to what her clients said without being aware of it. Some of her clients liked using visual speech, while others would use kinesthetic or auditory speech. This led them to believe that for a person, the highly regarded one sense more than the others and that they reflected that in words they used. When Satir would match what she said with the words her clients used, her clients felt as if she understood them. This would build rapport and made her interventions more easily accepted.

Bandler and Grinder found eye accessing cues, which are movements that the eyes make. They found that these movements could indicate if the person was using feelings, sounds and words, or pictures when they were learning, thinking, or remembering.

For example, when a person who is right-handed looks up and left, they are likely thinking about visual images. Then, after they studied Milton Erickson, they refined the language that therapists used to influence a person's actions.

NLP Pillars

NLP has four main pillars. The first pillar is rapport. NLP gives its practitioners the gift of being able to build a relationship with others. Rapport is basically being able to connect quickly with other people. It can be built quickly when you understand predicates, eye accessing cues, and modality preferences.

The second pillar is sensory awareness. When you walk into a person's house, you likely notice the sounds, smells, and colors that are subtly different than your home. NLP gives you the ability to notice that the world can be richer when you actually pay attention to all of your senses.

The third pillar is outcome thinking. The outcome of something is the goal that you want to achieve. Outcomes are connected to thinking about the things you want, as opposed to letting yourself be stuck in a bad mood of thinking. Using an outcome approach helps a person to make the best choices and decisions.

The fourth pillar is behavioral flexibility. This refers to being able to do things differently. Being flexible is one of the main aspects of using NLP. By learning NLP, you will gain a fresh perspective and will build new habits.

Tony Robbins

Today, NLP and Tony Robbins have become synonymous with each other. He has introduced more and more people to NLP than another teacher has. There are some who dismiss him as simply a showman, but considering how much he has accomplished, there is still a lot all of us could learn from him.

Tony Robbins has achieved so much success through NLP because he grabbed hold of its core concept of modeling and uses it whenever he gets the chance. He was even the student of John Grinder, and Grinder himself said that when the seminar he was teaching ended, Robbins came up to him and said he understood that modeling was the heart of NLP and was totally committed to modeling. He would then ask Grinder what he could undertake that would prove is commitment. Grinder said, firewalking. Tony Robbins is now famous for his firewalking ceremonies at his events.

At any of Robbins' seminars, you can witness him demonstrate his change techniques. Advanced students are able to spot the NLP techniques, but he also uses other patterns that he has come up with or has incorporated from various fields. One of the most important things that he demonstrates is his commitment to getting exactly what he wants, mainly moving a person into a place where they can access their inner resources.

The newcomer to NLP can learn a lot from Tony Robbin. The main way to learn from Robbins is by watching what he does aswell as listening to what he teaches. Observe the way he works. Observe how he moves. Observe the way he stands. Feel how intense he is. Hear the tone he uses. Basically, model him.

Tony Robbins is great at creating change in people, as well as marketing his products and himself, and for that, you will find it worthwhile to model him. The great thing is that his work has a specific structure, which makes it easy to emulate.

Chapter 2: Identify & Evaluate

What thoughts go through your head that make you feel down? These thoughts could be anxious, anger or guilt? Are you able to feel your thoughts? Aren't feelings and thoughts two different things? Don't we feel with the heart and think with the head?

Almost everybody will categorize feelings and thoughts in two different parts of the human mind. However, there is actually a closer relationship between those things than most people assume.

Feeling your thoughts doesn't happen in the same way that you feel, say, a poke on the arm. Instead, it means that you spot the connections between your feelings and thoughts. Behind every single emotion, there is a thought that triggered it. If you feel angry, what's the thought behind it? There has to be something or someone that has upset you. You aren't angry simply about nothing. Underlying that emotion is thoughts about being unfairly treated.

Emotions can't happen in a vacuum. Dig deep and figure out what thought is connected to those emotional responses. To do this, we need to look at some common thought triggers.

Different thoughts trigger different reactions. The following is an exercise that will help to test your knowledge of the connections between your feelings and thoughts. With each statement, you will pick if it is fearful, angering, depressive, guilt, or worrisome or anxious. To make it easier, you can label the feelings a, b, c, d, and e, respectively.

Number one, "I'm going to fall apart in that interview." Is that fearful, angering, depressive, guilt, or worrisome or anxious.

Number two, "I should have been a better parent." Is that fearful, angering, depressive, guilt, or worrisome or anxious.

Number three, "There's something very wrong with me." Is that fearful, angering, depressive, guilt, or worrisome or anxious.

Number four, "I can't stand it when people treat me this way." Is that fearful, angering, depressive, guilt, or worrisome or anxious.

Number five, "The world sucks, and I suck along with it." Is that fearful, angering, depressive, guilt, or worrisome or anxious.

Number six, "What if something bad happens and no one's there to help?" Is that fearful, angering, depressive, guilt, or worrisome or anxious.

Number seven, "I'm never good enough." Is that fearful, angering, depressive, guilt, or worrisome or anxious.

Number eight, "I have this feeling something terrible is going to happen." Is that fearful, angering, depressive, guilt, or worrisome or anxious.

You will use some of the emotions more than once. Now, try to match them up before reading anything further.

I'm trusting you answered them on your own first. The answers are fearful, guilt, depressive, angering, guilt, fearful, guilt, worrisome or anxious.

Let's go over some guidelines that can help you to classify a certain thought based on its emotional response.

1. Past vs Future

Anxious thoughts tend to have to do with an impending threat. Worry thoughts are caused by anticipating negative consequences, which are typically out of our control. Depressive or guilt thoughts often focus on previous disappointments and failures. The timeframe isn't a hard and fast rule because depressive thoughts can be caused by future events.

2. Others vs Self

Depressive thoughts normally have to do with the self, especially on the faults and what's lacking. Anger thoughts tend to come from perceptions of being treated badly by something or somebody.

3. Who I Am vs What I've Done

Depressive and guilt thoughts can be hard to differentiate, but a rule of thumb is that guilt thoughts have views of your own wrongdoings in certain situations. This often involves words like could, would, and should. Depressive thoughts are directed inward but focus on deficits and flaws and in yourself. Both are caused by exaggerated negative consequences and personal blame for bad events.

4. Something Bad

Fearful thoughts tend to come from dreaded consequences caused by a certain situation, place, or object. General anxiety involves worrisome thoughts and is kind of free-floating, a sense of apprehension that something bad is going to happen, or that there is something wrong.

The main thing with spotting triggers is "know the thought, know the emotion." Thoughts are always passing through your mind, one right after the other. However, there are some bad thoughts that keep coming up. What you need to do is grab the bad ones and place them in a category. Then you can figure out what deeper meaning it has for you.

Let's go over how you can catch a passing thought. This is the first step you have to take in restructuring your thought process. Once you have grabbed hold of a thought, start asking yourself these questions:

- Is this thought exaggerated or accurate?

- Does this thought help me, or is it bringing me down?

- Is there another way that I could be thinking about this?

- What would a say to a friend who had this thought?

- If I were thinking clearly, what might I say?

- What coping thoughts should I say to myself?

One way to catch an elusive thought is by using self-reflection. This means you take some time to reflect on what happened during the day. Start to connect your feelings to the things that have happened and with the thoughts that came with them. Did a person say something hurtful that left you upset or angry? Did what you had hope for not work out? Did something unexpected happen that had an unfortunate outcome? How did you end up feeling because of the things that did or did not happen? Or, had you been waiting for something positive to come along and are still waiting?

The main idea is for you to self-reflect through understanding the evens of the day and match your feelings to your thoughts that come up when you reflect on things. So, whenever you have a negative thought that was uninvited, try to grab hold of it and identify it.

A lot of people will want to know how they can push out all negative thoughts that pop up, but a lot like spitting in the wind, trying to focus your mind on forcing out these negative thoughts will backfire because those thoughts will become more prominent. Substituting your thought processes isn't the same as forcing yourself not to have negative thoughts. It's simply a way to overwriting the negative script you have by substituting it with healthier thoughts. When you have realized that a negative thought is simply an opinion, and it isn't a fact and doesn't have control over you, the thoughts will start to fade.

Chapter 3: The Power of the Subconscious Mind

Dr. Maxel Maltz, a New York plastic surgeon, wrote a book entitled *Psychocybernetics*. In his books, he talks about how powerful the subconscious mind in controlling the opinions we have about ourselves. He talks about the stories of people who asked him for various different surgeries. Some of them had big noses, some had been in an accident that left them disfigured, and others wanted to reverse what age had done.

There are some patients who loved the results. But others, even though they had great results, still thought they were ugly. Dr. Maltz finally realized that those who still hated how they looked had programmed these negative thoughts into their subconscious mind. Those thoughts of "I'm ugly," were the dominant thoughts in their minds.

The subconscious is where every memory, event, and incident is stored. For the most part, you aren't consciously aware of what is going on, but that doesn't mean it has no effect on you. In fact, it has more effect on you than your conscious mind. If you have a horrible teacher that made fun of you for your intelligence, it is going to leave an imprint on your subconscious. If something goes wrong and it causes you to feel like a failure, that will leave a mark as well. When you experience something similar to that now, all of those negative imprints will show up and will control how you react to it.

For the most part, you won't even realize why you have that response. This is how powerful your subconscious is. There are lots of different programming in your mind that is either negative or positive. All of them have been put there by you, and it will bubble up and affect different situations.

When the subconscious impacts you in some way, you won't be aware of it, but the way you act will clue you in on this. So, to figure out if your subconscious mind is affecting you negatively, see if you can spot these clues.

1. Thinking in Black and White

When you see only extremes, this isn't a normal thought pattern. Most of life is full of grays. Relationships, jobs, people, and such are made up of some black, some white, and several in-between. For example, if you see everybody as good or bad, then you aren't seeing them in reality. The subconscious is superimposing itself based on things from your past. A person could have a certain negative personality trait that reminds you of somebody who has treated you badly. You are projecting your experiences onto the new person.

2. You have Mood Swings Often

While having large mood swings is a sign of bi-polar, this is different. Let's say that you are in a good mood and then somebody says, "Are you okay? You look tired." This throws you into a tailspin, and your mood drops. This isn't a mood swing that a person with rational thought would have. This is caused by your subconscious reminding you of something.

3. You have Bad Habits

These habits tend to be a type of escapism. Some painful things have happened in the past. You might actually remember them, but, consciously, you feel incapable, unloved, unworthy, and so on. To feel better, you shop, overeat, become a couch potato, drink, and so on. This will only help to reinforce those negative thoughts that live within your subconscious.

4. You Constantly Think and Speak about the Future or Past

People with positive outlooks will live in the now. Their focus is on today, the things they want to accomplish, thinking about, and starting. Focusing on the future or past will typically come from the subconscious programming that makes you think that you were happier in the past or you are going to be happier in the future. You aren't able to be happy in the present because you have a lot of negative things happening.

5. You have Fears, Worries, and Anxieties

There are times when we don't know where our fears or worries come from. We let small problems paralyze us, or we have generalized anxiety. We start worrying about things that haven't even happened.

6. You are Judgmental of Others and Your Self

Once our subconscious mind has been programmed with the beliefs that we are incapable, flawed, and stupid, then we view others and ourselves in that light. Nothing is good enough, and all we see are the negative parts of our situations. We are always on the lookout for those negatives so that we can reinforce our beliefs.

Limiting Beliefs

These negative subconscious thoughts that we have are what is known as limiting beliefs. They constrain in some way. By simply believing these thoughts, we choose not to think, speak, or do the things that they inhibit. This hurts our life. Limiting beliefs tend to do with our self-identity and ourselves. Some of the beliefs could also involve the world, decisions we want to make and other people.

We can define ourselves with things we do or don't do. If you simply say, "I am..." this could mean that you simply believe that, and you don't fully market yourself as such. On the other side of things, you can also judge yourself with the things that you don't think you should get, so you don't seek out those things.

Then we can have beliefs about the things we can and can't do. If you believe that you can't sing, then you may not try or take singing lessons to try to improve your singing. This is the main problem with "I can't" statements; they cause us to believe that our abilities are completely fixed.

The next type of limiting belief is I must or I mustn't. We tend to be controlled by laws, norms, values, and other rules that cause constraints in the things we must not do. However, not every single one of these is mandatory, and many of them are very limiting.

The verb "to be" can cause quite a lot of problems because while you can think "I am," it also means you can think "I am not." For example, if you think that you are an artist, it may also make you think that you can't be good at math. Thinking using "I am" assumes that we are not able to change. No matter if the thought is positive or negative, saying "I am" will automatically stop your thinking. It can also cause generalization.

We can also have limiting beliefs about other people, which can limit us in various ways. If we believe that another person is more capable than we are, then we won't challenge them. If we view them as selfish, we probably won't ask them for help. People often use the "theory of mind" to guess what others are thinking about them. Most of these guesses are wrong. A lot of people will jump to the conclusion that somebody doesn't like them when they likely haven't formed an opinion.

Then we also have limiting beliefs about how the world works. This can include things like the property of materials to the laws of nature. This could cause you to believe that every dog will bite you or think that traveling by airplane is dangerous.

People still question whether or not limiting beliefs are bad or if they can actually help us from getting hurt. In practice, there are some limiting beliefs that are valid beliefs that are worth keeping. This issue is trying to spot the good ones from the bad ones. Most people will err on the side of possible safety. This means we play into the erroneous limiting beliefs that cause us to act with undue caution.

NLP can help you to work through those negative thought processes. But the best advice I can give you about changing your negative thoughts is to keep the positive ones simple. When you are faced with a challenge, there is no need to think about every single little detail of what might go wrong, or how the deadline isn't long enough. The thoughts you actually need are simple. Things like, "I can do it. I am capable and bright." If your relationship dissolves, keep things simple. "That relationship wasn't the right one for me. I am worthy of an amazing relationship."

Chapter 4: Law of Attraction

One truth of the law of attraction is that it is always working and is a powerful law. Like gravity, it is constantly in motion. It works in your life every single moment. You are always creating. Every moment of every day, you are creating your reality. Every thought you have, whether subconscious or conscious, is creating your future. You can't turn it off.

Understanding exactly how the law of attraction works will help you to change your life, and give you the power to create your best future. The law of attraction gives you an infinite number of possibilities, joy, and abundance. It isn't difficult to use, and it is able to change every aspect of your life.

The simplest explanation of the law of attraction is that you will attract the things you focus on. The things you give your attention and energy to will end up coming back to you. If you remain focused on positive and good things that happen in your life, you are going to start attracting more positive and good things. If you instead focus on negativity and the bad in life, then that is what you are going to get back.

The basic principle is like attracts like. When you feel abundant, appreciative, joyful, happy, passionate, enthusiastic, or excited, then you send out that same positive energy. But, if you are feeling sad, resentful, angry, stressed out, anxious, or bored, then you send that negative energy out.

Before I was using the law of attraction I understood the concept of it but I never actually applied it in life because I didn't think it was true. Anyway, I started using it in my life and it started working so now I use it religiously.

The law of attraction will respond with enthusiasm with all of those vibrations. It doesn't pick the ones that would be best for you. It simply gives you back exactly what you have sent out. Since your vibrations will attract the same frequencies, it is important that you work on sending out feelings, energy, and thoughts that resonate with the things that you want to experience, do, and be.

First off, always ask for what you want and not for the things you don't want. This is why it is important for you to be deliberate about the things you feel and think so that the Universe isn't responding to a bunch of random things. So, figure out what it is that you would like to receive in life. And while you are doing this, work on feeling the emotions that you will experience once you have that item. Ask yourself, "How would I feel if I got this?" "What would I do?" "What would life look like if I got this or this happened" The more you focus on the things you do want, the faster you are going to get your goals and dreams.

Next, you have to believe that you are going to get exactly what you want and then do something to make it happen. Believing it will happen means keeping a positive expectancy, and go about your day with absolute certainty. You have just put your future into powerful hands. This isn't always all that easy. Limiting beliefs can create problems with this part. Once you are able to believe that you will get the things that you want, the second part of this is taking inspired action. These actions will help you to reach the goals you want. The Universe may be helping you, but that doesn't mean you don't have to do any work on your part.

If you're reminded of something by seeing it, hearing it, speaking it then eventually it will come, as long as you put it the correct action towards getting there.

Next, work to match your vibrations with what you want. One of the easiest ways to do this is to focus on creating positivity throughout the day. You can also take the time to focus on the emotions that you would feel once your goal has arrived. You can use dream boards; post-it notes that you place in places you see often, change your screensaver to something that represents your goal, and so on. This will take some effort, but the more you do it and practice it, the easier it will be.

One of the most popular things people will use to attract is money is visualizing getting checks in the mail, having an inspired monthly income goal on your phone screen saver, and even having 100 dollar notes on your bathroom mirror. You can also write yourself a check for the amount of money that you would like to manifest this year and keep it in your wallet. Make sure that you take a moment each day to be thankful for the things you have.

When it comes to bringing love into your life, focus on love. Become the love that you would like to attract. Start to become more generous and loving with yourself and others. When you create this vibration, it will draw love to you.

Something that will help you, no matter what you are trying to manifest, is gratitude. Gratitude is its own form of abundance. Being grateful each day is fairly easy. All you need is to write down three to ten things you are grateful for each day. This will automatically put you in alignment with gratitude and will help you to attract more things to be grateful for into your life.

It's easy for us to fall into the negatives first, but start your day with everything you're happy and grateful for.

Chapter 5: NLP Training

In this first chapter with NLP exercises, we will be looking at techniques towards changing your negative beliefs or experiences in life into something that is positive. Before you start using any of these techniques, make sure you know exactly what you want to change. It is also a good idea to read through the actual techniques completely before starting. It's important that you know what you are supposed to do. Some of these can seem very complicated, but they aren't once you understand the basics. That's why we will start with memory manipulation and submodalities.

Memory Manipulation

This first NLP technique is going to be so obvious that once you have figured it out, you will be shocked at the number of people who aren't in control of it. One of my friends hit me with a bombshell one day. She told me she had a phobia of worms. This isn't a very common phobia to hear about, and for most people, it doesn't make much sense. You don't hear a lot about being tragically affected by worms, thus scarring them for life. But, I asked her why she was so scared of worms because I couldn't picture it my head.

She explained that whenever she was working in her garden, she would picture herself pulling the trowel up, and with it would be a worm. The worm wouldn't be a normal-sized one, but one that was probably more the size of a small snake. She could imagine its sliminess, and as she lifted the trowel up, she would see the worm flick upwards and come flying up at her face, leaving her covered in its slime. Sometimes, she would see it ending up in her mouth.

With that visualization, I could totally see why she was afraid of worms. While all of this only ever happened in her mind, this idea was so horrible that she seriously believed that this could happen when she dug in her garden.

Something to learn from this is that the brain isn't all the clever, and for others, it isn't even that clever. The brain isn't even able to tell the difference between what happens in your head or what happens in real life. My friend reacted simply from an idea of a worm flying at her just like it would have reacted had it actually happened. But, the good news is that you change what's on the inside.

What if my friend, instead of picturing that horrible worm flying at her, saw a worm come out of the ground, smile at her, thank her, and then move along? Do you think she'd still be afraid of them? Do you think that the new image would be any less valid than the old one?

No, on both counts. There is a chance, though, that if she makes the image too cute, she may start digging up the garden in the hopes of finding worms. Before we dive into the actual technique, we need to go over some NLP elements.

1. When you think of a memory, you will remember the representations of the sense you used when it happened.

2. You will remember the things you saw, heard, felt (on the inside and outside), smelled, and tasted.

For the most part, you only need to use three of those five senses. This is what is known as the modalities, and the three that you need are kinesthetic, visual, and auditory modalities. Whenever you do think up memory, you only remember a representation of it. You aren't actually remembering what happened. You remember what happened, but after it has been filtered through your beliefs.

In a sense, you remember things that happened in a way that gives you the change to not have to question the things you believe about yourself. If you think that doesn't have any confidence and remember a person saying something strange before rudely walking away, you will probably think that it's all your fault because you are boring, not because you intimidated them. You came to the conclusion that matched up with the beliefs you have about yourself.

Let's begin.

Start by thinking about a person who makes you feel uncomfortable, somebody who causes you to feel insignificant and small, a person who you have a hard time dealing with, someone you have a hard time communication with, or a person who always seems to have the upper hand. Now, start to think about having to deal with them in the near future. At this moment, you are probably creating a picture of this person in your mind. If you aren't, or if you are struggling to come up with that image, then think of a picture of them instead. What type of image have you come up with?

Now, if this image was real, what part of it would make you uncomfortable? If the person is a lot bigger than you in your image, that would be the scary part. If they talk very loudly, that would be scary. If they have a nasty scowl on their fact, that would be scary as well.

If a boxer, before his fight, pictured himself facing his opponent, but the opponent was 12 feet tall, I'm guessing he would be lacking in confidence when the fight actually comes around.

Normally, you will have something unrealistic about the image you come up with, something that makes it scary. There are a lot of ways to change how this image came to make you feel, and we will look at that in the submodalities sections, but we are just going to look at the "content" of your memory.

So, your first step is to think about a time when you will be facing the person who bothers you and try to figure out what the unrealistic part of it is, and then turn it realistic. For example, if the person is really tall, bring them down to normal sign.

One by one, start to change all of those unrealistic parts into realistic parts.

Now, we are going to take things a bit further and make other things unrealistic. Zoom in on their face and push a big red clown's nose on their face. How do they seem now? What happens if you add a clown hat and suit? What about big shoes? Do they still seem as scary? What is going on?

When you see a person with a clown's nose, you typically don't take them seriously, and this is what you are doing right now in your head. This is a type of generalization. We have the generalization that a clown's nose means the person shouldn't be taken seriously.

If you have a fear of clowns, then this probably won't work well for you, so please choose something else. Other good choices are minor celebrities, cartoon characters, and WWE wrestlers.

There are a lot of people who may have come across something similar to this before, like nervous speakers imagining their audience naked. Making a change to memory, especially in a humorous manner, can make a big difference to your state of mind.

This will work for other modalities as well, so up next, we will do that for the auditory modality.

Take a moment to scour your memory for a person who bothers you and has an annoying voice. This should be a voice that causes you to cringe, sounds like a dental drill, or is overpowering. Now, what will happen if you change up how their voice sounds?

If the person you thought of had an authoritative and deep voice, what happens when you give them Donald Duck's voice? Speeding up a person's voice until they start to sound like chipmunks is another great option. If a person tends to tire you out because of their voice, then trying slowing them down.

Now, we are going to put all of this together. Think about five people who you have had problems dealing with in the past. Imagine the next time you are going to have to face them. Using both the auditory and visual hallucinations, make them so that they are easier to face. Here are some visual things you could do:

- Put a mustache on them, especially great if it's a woman

- Put them in a dress, especially if it's a man

- Give them a bad haircut

- Make them so they can't stand up

- Dress them up like Shirley Temple

- Dress them up like a clown.

Here are some auditory choices:

- Add in a funny soundtrack to the memory – Benny Hill is a good option

- Helium

- Make them sound like Donald Duck or Sylvester the cat

The more you use these techniques, the easier they will be to use. It will also help you to become more aware of the different things your brain does to make a memory seem bad. There are some people who find changing one modality works well enough for them, and some people can't make this one work for them. That's why there are so many different NLP techniques.

This can also be used for phobias. Maybe you could think of a spider wearing striped leggings in roller skates.

Submodalities

In the last technique, we learned to change the way we see and hear something we didn't like. Now we are going to look at how to change submodalities. Submodalities are used to compliment your content changes and gives you a basis for other NLP techniques.

We will be changing the structure of memory. I want you to start thinking about a time when it was sunny, and you were having a great time outside. Really concentrate on the image that you create, and make sure that you remember this as if you were actually there. This means you can't see yourself, but you are seeing everything through your eyes. This means you are associated with the memory.

Really concentrate on this and notice the feelings this image is evoking. Next, we will change up the structure of this memory just to see what it will do.

When it comes to NLP, each of the five modalities has several different submodalities. For example, the modality of vision has five submodalities:

- Contrast

- Location

- Brightness

- Size

- Distance

The difference in changing a memory's content and changing its structure is like a television set. When you change the structure it's like changing the speed of the picture, contrast, color level, or brightness instead of changing what's on the screen.

The biggest problem with working on submodalities is that people can get confused between the content and submodalities. Let's look at a few examples.

Picture an image floating in space that is about arm's length from you. The picture is about the size of a TV screen and is made up of you on the beach on a sunny day. When you change the submodality of the location, you would change the position of the image to the right, left, down, up, backward, forwards, or any mixture of these without actually changing the picture.

When you change the size, it means that the picture stays in the same place, but you enlarge it or shrink it.

Changing up the brightness can be hard, depending on what your picture is because it is hard to not change up the actual content. Picture yourself making an image of a candlelit dinner brighter. Changing the brightness, in this case, might not be useful, but several exercises, brightness is very important.

Alright, so let's go back to that image of something that makes you feel really good. Really imagine this picture and notice where in space it is located. Now imagine yourself pushing the picture off into the distance. It stays the same size, but it is moving further away, so it will appear smaller.

What does this do to how you feel about the memory?

Now pull the image back towards you, not as close as it originally was, but close enough that you can see it clearly. How does this make you feel? Take the image back to where it originally was.

A lot of people will say that when the picture is closer, they feel stronger, and when they push it away, it lessens this feeling. This works just the same no matter if the memory is negative or positive. If this is how you felt, then great. If not, don't worry about it. While it may be a common response, it doesn't mean everybody will feel it.

Alright, we are going to take that image you have, that happy image, and work through each of the submodalities. Before you start on the next submodality, make sure you place the image back in the original position and likeness.

1. Make the image brighter. How does that make you feel? Make the image dimmer. How does that make you feel?

2. Move the image away from you, and then move it closer to you. How did you feel?

3. Put the color in black and white. How does this feel? Now enhance the colors in the picture. How do you feel about this?

4. Unfocus the image and make it blurry. How do you feel? Sharpen the image. How does this feel?

5. Change the size of the image, making it smaller and then bigger than before. How did this make you feel?

6. Add some movement to the image and then make the image completely still. How did these make you feel?

7. Place a border around the image and then make it a panoramic view so that it fills your view. How do you feel?

8. Picture the image through your eyes. How does this feel? Now, see yourself inside the image. How does this feel?

Something you may have noticed is that some of the shifts work differently than the others. The first shifts you made were analog, meaning there was an infinite number of ways to change in the picture, such as how far away it is from you, whereas with the association, you are either in the image or not.

Now, I need you to figure out a memory from your past that is extremely positive, but sound plays a big part in it. This might be a certain person's voice, or it could be the sound of the waves on the beach. The main thing is that the memory has a strong auditory element, and it elicits a positive emotional response.

Like we did before, we are going to work through a list of submodalities, but for sound this time, and change them up. Take note of how each of these changes makes you feel and make sure before you do the next that you take the picture back to original.

1. Turn the volume down in the memory, and then turn the volume way up in the memory. How did these changes feel?

2. Reduce the tones of the sounds, and then increase the tone of the sounds. How does this make you feel?

3. Slow all of the sounds down, and then speed all of the sounds way up. How did this make you feel?

4. Reduce the pitch of your sounds, and then raise the pitch. How did this make you feel?

5. Then switch up the position in space where the sounds are coming from. Try many different positions to which ones make the most difference.

Now, what can you do with all of this information? The best way to explain that is through an example. Let's say that you have a memory that makes you feel uncomfortable. You have the choice to use what we did in the last technique, or you can change the intensity of the submodalities.

Maybe you found that changing the brightness changed the way you felt about something, like making the image brighter made the feelings more intense. Maybe you could try reducing the brightness on an uncomfortable memory and see if it makes you feel better towards it. It probably will, but there is a chance that when you stop actively thinking about it, the image will go back to the original.

So, how do you make it stay? There are a lot of options, but the simplest is to continually change the image until it stays. The faster you can do it, the better it will stick.

Dissolving Bad Memories

This NLP technique will use a combination of what we have already learned. This will help to dissolve any bad memories you may have. Before you begin, make sure you are in a quiet place where you can relax and not be disturbed. This may take a while, so make sure you have a decent amount of time set aside for this.

Next, bring up an image of a bad experience you have had. This is probably going to be something that you have had pop up in your mind time and time again, that isn't helpful. This could be an embarrassing moment, or it could be a traumatizing experience.

If you need to, you can close your eyes to this. Most people find it easier to imagine things when their eyes are closed.

Now, focus on the auditory and visual aspects of this memory. What are the things that you can see? Are there any other people in the memory? What are the things that you hear?

Tune into the things that you are able to see. What types of colors are in the scene? What types of things are around you? How close are things? Are they big or small? What about this memory that makes you feel bad?

Now, start to push those things further away. Push them so far out that they are on the horizon. Make all of the colors muted and pale. Now, what are some good things that you can learn from this bad memory? Grab hold of the good things and keep hold of them as you blow all of the other parts of the memory away.

Now, pull the sounds of this memory back up. If you need the image again, that's okay. Now, make all of those sounds muffled, further away, and quieter. Notice if there are any sounds that can help those good lessons you grabbed hold become stronger. Take those good sounds and hold onto them. Now, imagine a thunderstorm drowning out all of those bad memories sounds.

If this memory pops back into your mind in the future, all you need to do is this visualization again. The more you do it, the more it will stick.

Explode Bad Memories

This works like the last one, but instead of watching the bad memories dissolve, this one explodes them. Once you learn this one, you can decide which one of these techniques work best for you.

Like before, make sure you have plenty of time to do this and find a place where you feel comfortable and can relax. Bring the bad memory to mind that you would like to get rid of. Bad memories typically don't serve you in any way, and they tend to plague your thoughts and pop at the most inopportune moments. Why does this memory keep coming to mind?

Now, focus on all of the modalities of this memory. What types of things are around you? Are there other people involved? Are you inside or outside? What types of sounds do you hear? Is there music playing? Are there nature sounds? Can you taste anything in this memory? Are you touching anything or anything that you can touch? Are you moving around, or can you?

Now start to change the submodalities of these things. Try making the sounds louder, colors brighter, and so on. Think about the things that the experience taught you. Take hold of those lessons, and don't let them go.

Continue to make all of the submodalities stronger and stronger in your memory. Make things bigger, brighter, bolder, more vivid, louder, until everything explodes away. The only that is left behind is the lesson that you learned from the experience.

Any time you feel that you need to, you can repeat this technique.

Curing Phobias

This is considered a "fast" phobia cure, but it can take people several days to several weeks to months to actually cure their phobia. That said, it is an effective way to overcome phobias, especially those that are interfering with your quality of life. This technique is made up of three sections.

In the first section, you will access your phobia in a safe environment. All you need to do is be in a safe place where you won't be disturbed and then close your eyes. In your mind's eye, set up an imaginary movie cinema and take as much time as you need. Get creative and have fun with this.

Once you are ready, walk to the front of the cinema and take a seat in the very front row in one of the most comfortable and luxurious seats. Make sure you get really good and relaxed in those seats.

Once you feel ready, picture yourself leaving your body, still relaxed in the seat that you picked, and float all the way up to the balcony and take another seat that is just as comfortable. Now you should be able to see yourself in the front row staring at the screen, and you can screen as well.

As you watch both of these things, place the first colored picture of the movie of your phobia on the screen. Let this movie of your phobia run in color. Stop it once it gets to the last slide and then switch the coloring to a dull and muted grey so that you are only able to see the content that is on that slide.

Now, we will move into the second section. In this section, you will replay your phobia with some happy emotions. Pick a piece of music or a song that elicits happy emotions from you. Now, float yourself into that muted grey slide and allow yourself to associate with the end of your phobia movie once you have recovered from seeing your phobia.

Once you are ready, start to play your movie backward at twice the speed that it was while you play your favorite song in your head and be completely associated with the phobia. Once you reach the beginning of the movie, freeze it again and make sure that it is still in that muted grey color.

You may need to repeat this section of this task as many times as you need, making the movie move faster each time. The goal is to make you less afraid of your phobia as possible.

In the last section, you will disassociate from your phobia. You need to float out of the picture again and place yourself back in your body that is still sitting at the front of the cinema. Take note of how comfortable the seat is and then take the picture off of the screen so that it is white.

Once you feel you are ready to watch your phobia movie in color all the through, do so. As you do so, make sure that you stay completely aware of how comfortable that seat is that you are sitting in. If you don't feel that you are ready for this step, then go back to the very beginning and start over. You can do those first two sections as many times as you need to. Only move onto this third section when you are absolutely certain that you can handle it.

Once you do feel like doing this third section, watch the movie of your phobia while focusing on your comfortable seat. This disassociates you from your actual phobia, and you might be quite surprised at how different it feels now to see your phobia.

As always, you can repeat this technique as often as you need to, and you can use it for as many phobias as you have.

Chapter 6: NLP (Higher Level of Thinking)

In this section of NLP techniques, we will go over exercises that will improve your thinking process with yourself and your communication process with other people. Getting rid of negative memories and thoughts is only half the battle. You have to make sure that you communicate with yourself in the best way possible because that tends to be our downfall as humans. We put on a happy face for everybody else, but inside we are beating ourselves up over something that isn't even important. Using NLP will help you to create more positive and helpful self-talk.

Something that some people find controversial about NLP is the fact that you can use it to influence other people. It can be used to build rapport with people, which can be the hardest process of building a relationship. When we go over those exercises, don't look at them as ways to manipulate people because they're not. They are simple tools to help let another person know that you care and are listening to them because, after all, that's all humans ask for.

Meta Programs

Meta programs, also known as NLP profiles, are sensory filters that everybody has. People express the profiles through the things they say. When you learn meta programs, it will help you to understand others as well as yourself better.

We all have various preferences for the language we use. We are going to look at five important NLP meta-programs so that you can figure out what your preferences are and start to become more aware of other people's preferences. Then we will look at how we can use this information to motivate and influence others and ourselves.

In each of these groups, pick the set of words that resonate with you the most. You may also be somewhere in between.

- Motivation

    - Right away, just do it, get it done, jump in, do it

    - Learn more, find out, analyze, wait, think about it

    - If you prefer the first set, you are on the "active" side, and if the second set is more you, you are more "reactive."

- Motivational Direction

    - Outcome, achieve, get, have, obtain, attain

    - So we don't have to, get rid of, solve, eliminate, prevent, avoid

    - If you chose the first set, you are on the "towards" side, and if you chose the second set, you are on the "away from" side.

- Motivational Source

    - You just know

    - Others notice others tell you, feedback

    - If you feel like you just know, then you're "internally referenced." If you have to have external validation or feedback, then you are "externally referenced."

- Motivational Choice

    - Do it differently, break the rules, lots of choice, possibilities, variety, opportunity

    - Procedures, first... second... third, the right way

    - If you connect with the first set, you side with the "options," and if you like the second set, you like "procedures."

- Working Organization

    o People I know, relationships, thoughts, feelings, people's names

    o What I did, processes, goals, things, systems, tasks

    o If you like the first set, you are people orientated, and if you liked the second set, you are task orientated.

So, why are these profiles helpful? Well everybody tends to be influenced more by one set than the other; very few falls in between. This could also mean that your brain doesn't even consciously pick up the other set of words. When we use the words that relate to use more, it's more likely that we are going to listen to what we have to say.

The way to make sure that this happens is to, every now and then, use the exact words that the other person uses, with a matching tone as well. When you are trying to figure out what side another person falls on, you can use words from both groups until things become clearer. Let's take the "motivational level" section. You could begin by saying, "We've carefully thought about this, we've analyzed the information, and we want to jump in and do it."

The more that you are able to align yourself with another person's preferences, the more likely they will listen to you, and the more you will be able to influence them.

Amplify Good Feelings

This technique uses submodalities and anchors to help amplify your good feelings and lock them into place so that you are able to access them whenever you need to. In NLP, an anchor is a trigger or stimulus that you pair with a certain response. You have already established a lot of anchors because they can be covert, open, inadvertent, and deliberate.

Alright, to begin this, you will need to find a quiet and relaxing place where you won't be disturbed for a while. Make sure you are comfortable, and you can fully focus on your task at hand.

Now, in your mind, bring up an amazing experience you have had. Place yourself inside of that memory. Picture everything that you saw, everything that you heard, all of the smells you smelled, and the things you felt.

Begin to intensify all of those feelings, sounds, sights, and smells. Continue to make then closer, stronger, brighter, and bigger. Experiment around with these changes and figure out which ones make that memory even better for you. Do this until you find the point where everything is maximized to their fullest effect.

Figure out where in your body, all of these good feelings are coming from. Follow this good feeling all the way through your body. Make these good feelings stronger, faster, and bigger until you are completely bathed in this good feeling.

Next, you need to anchor these feelings to something, some action, or movement. You can pick what you want, or you can do what I'm going to suggest. Once you are completely bathed in all of those good feelings, press the tip of your index figure and thumb together and push all of those good feelings into that movement.

In the future, whenever you start feeling down and you need a pick-me-up, all you have to is press your index figure and thumb together, and all of those good feelings will come flooding into you again.

Modeling

This is the most important NLP skill and works to help you connect with other people. You will have to test out things because only through testing will your modeling abilities be able to be improved.

Just like with any other NLP technique, you need to first think about what it is that you are looking to achieve. The three main goals of modeling include:

1. Creating techniques that will improve performance.

2. Modeling bad actions so that we can learn the things that we need to change or avoid.

3. Use modeling to better understand and know a person. The more you know how a person thinks, the easier it is going to be to build rapport.

One truth that remains is that if you want to learn something, ask, and then watch. After that, you can use these steps, test them, and then improve them. Then you will be well on your way to becoming a good modeler.

1. Ask

There are times in life when we make things too difficult. If you want to learn how to do a particular thing, find somebody who can and then ask them how they do it. To test this, can you make it work for you? If you aren't able to do so, then continue to the next step.

2. Using NLP Techniques

This will use meta-models and specific questions that will help to identify the sensory sequence that brings you to a certain result. When you ask these questions, certain points will become obvious, which will give you an easy change.

One of the best ways to become good at this is constantly practicing meta-models and elicitation questions. NLP really is all about practicing. Some of the best elicitation questions are:

"How do you know?"

"Tell me more."

"What does that mean?"

"What happened next?"

"What happened before that?"

You may find yourself repeating these questions, as well. Doing this will allow you to find anchors and triggers that will provide you with key information to help discourage or encourage certain actions.

3. Pure NLP Modeling

This is also a type of "deep trance identification." To begin, you will need to pick a success model. This is where you choose a person who has skills that you would like to improve and explore. It's very important that you have gotten to see them do what it is that you want to model, whether on video or in real life. The more you are able to listen and watch them in a neutral state, the better things will go.

Then you will imagine them performing. Sit in a comfortable place and close your eyes. Imagine listening and watching this person perform the action. Let this movie play in your mind and picture yourself building rapport with that person as they perform.

Then picture yourself floating into them. Play that movie through again as if you were them. They will do all of the work, but you will feel, hear, and see what they feel, hear, and see.

Move back into your body. As you are leaving them, take everything that you have learned that is useful for you to use now or at some time in the future. Then, in your mind, play that movie again, but this time, you are the main character, doing everything that you want to learn.

Do this once or twice more. This will help you to become more comfortable with the action.

Now, you need to break the state. For example, stare at the floor and take note of all of the textures in the flooring and then go back to doing what you want to.

Next, find a safe place to practice the skill you want to learn. Continue to practice and take in all of your useful information.

You can repeat this entire process as many times as you need to.

There are other NLP modeling techniques, but I feel that these are the best for beginners to start with.

Self Compassion

This is a great technique to use whenever you are feeling stressed or anxious. When you do this exercise, there is a chance that abreaction will occur. Abreaction is the release of repressed emotion. This means you could experience a large purge of emotions that you had long forgotten about. This isn't a bad thing. This is actually a really good thing but only move forward with this exercise if you are okay with that happening.

It is very important that you are in a comfortable and safe place where you will not be disturbed.

Think about five different characters that you view positively. This might be a childhood toy, a pet, a friend, family members, anything, and anybody. The important thing is to make sure that it is something that you respect.

Next, bring up any anxiety and put yourself inside of that worry. Allow yourself to be totally immersed in it. Describe this worry using as many senses as you are able to and create a completely honest description of the way that you feel.

Allow yourself to relax and picture the millions of people all over the world who are experiencing that same feeling. Everybody has felt anxious or worried at some point, so think about them.

With them, send them all compassionate waves of good wishes. Then, picture them wishing you well, too.

Now, bring those five characters you thought about earlier to mind and allow them to surround you. Picture them saying things to you like: "Be kind to yourself. Take care of yourself and nurture yourself. Be kind, care, nurture..." Continue to repeat those same words to yourself and take in all of those compassionate and nurturing thoughts.

Once you have finished doing this, check-in to see how you are feeling. Are there any changes? Accept whatever you are feeling and don't question it. Take note of something, no matter how small, that you are able to do to make yourself feel better in the future.

Bring yourself back into the present moment and then take that lesson with you.

Humans tend to be very self-critical. This exercise helps you to restore some balance into your life and helps to improve your mental health.

Building Rapport

We have talked about a few things already that can help you to build rapport with people, but we are going to go over a few more specifics. Building rapport basically means that you are increasing how many similarities you have with another person to help them relax and feel as if they can relate to you.

Obviously, we can only work on the elements that we actually have control over, but there are quite a few areas where you can build rapport. For example, if two people like the same football team, or are the same race, religion, or sex, then they already have a pretty good head start. Other ways to help build rapport is to match:

- Physical movements

- Physical posture

- Emotions

- Sensory language

- Voice volume, tone, and rhythm

- Breath rate

One of the best ways to improve this skill is to choose a single element and then practice matching it in different situations where you are able to relax and don't have to concentrate on other things. This could be if you are on the subway or in line at the grocery store.

Simply try to mimic another person that is close to you. One of the best ways to know if you have been successful is if they all of a sudden notice you standing there. The more you practice this, the better you are going to get at it.

One quick note on breath matching, if you want to match up with somebody's breath, the way to do it is not by staring at their chest. The best thing you can do is to use your peripheral vision. Nobody is going to buy the excuse of practicing your rapport skills for getting caught staring at their chests.

You should stand or sit next to them, with your eyes facing forward, take your awareness to your peripheral vision. You will notice that it is a lot easier to notice their movements that way. This is because peripheral vision deals with movement specifically.

In general, you will discover that certain elements that you match with are going to have a bigger effect and that some type of combination will be easier to use than other combinations. Combining posture matching and matching breaking is something that you should work on.

Pacing and Leading

The next logical thing to learn, once you have gotten the hang of building rapport, is pacing and leading. Pacing is simply your building rapport with somebody. Leading is what you do after you have achieved rapport.

For example, if a friend comes to you really angry, you can start by matching their breath, gestures, and loud voice and then begin to lower your voice and slow down your breathing to see if they follow suit.

Hypnotists use leads as well, the most common being leading the client into a trance. If a hypnotist were to try to hypnotize a person and not be relaxed when they do it, they are going to find it impossible to get the other person hypnotized. It is very important to be aware of your own state.

One of the hardest parts about pacing and leading is knowing exactly when you should start leading and how quickly you should switch state. It won't work to match the person's angry mood and automatically change to catatonic. This isn't going to do anything, except maybe cause your friend to question if you are alright.

Once you are positive that you have built rapport, then you should change your breathing just slightly. If they don't switch with you, then go back to matching theirs. Continue to make these little steps until you have reached the results that you want. Like with most skills, pacing and leading are going to become automatic the more you do it.

Sensory Language

Have you ever heard two people having a conversation where their words make sense, but they don't seem to accept or understand their statements? One of the main elements at play is the way that people translate the actual speech to their internal views of the moment. Here's an example.

Sales Associate: "How can I help you today?"

This is an okay opening because it gets rid of the "no" option than simply asking, "Can I help you?" will create.

Customer: "I want to get a new CD player. Can you show me what you have?"

While this may sound like a straight forward statement, you need to pay attention to the visual language that they use. These are words like show.

Sales Associate: "I have the new Sony. It has a really nice bass, and the trebles are pretty good. Would you like to hear it?"

The associate is focused on the sense that is most important to him, and when it comes to CD players, that would be sound, so saying it "sounds" good seems right to him when talking about audio equipment.

Customer: "Could I look at it?"

How often do you think a person purchases a new sound system based simply on how it looks instead of how it sounds? It happens more often than you would believe.

Customer: "Looks nice, but it also looks expensive. I feel uncomfortable having to spend that much."

The customer is still focused on the looks, but they need to feel right in order to make a decision. The decision the customers make will always be based on their feeling.

Sales Associate: "Yes, it does, but if you listen to how it sounds, you would be able to hear the quality of it."

I am assuming that you don't really need any more explanation, and hopefully, you have come to realize just how annoyed the customer could end up becoming at this point.

This could be a better option for the associate.

Sales Associate: "How can I help you today?"

Customer: "I want to get a new CD player. Can you show me what you have?"

Sales Associate: "I have the new Sony. They look amazing and modern. Its lights are also subtle. It's not that cheap, but you do sometimes have to pay more in order to get better quality and longer lasting products."

That will work better. You need to talk about things that will work into the internal representation that the other person has made, and it also gets rid of the object about the cost.

Customer: "It does look nice. It seems expensive. I feel uncomfortable about having to spend that much."

Sales Associate: "Yes, it is a bit more expensive, but you're paying for a better finish. The cheaper options tend to wear out faster, with scuff marks and fingerprints. Imagine, in five years, how amazing you will feel because this will still look just as new and shiny as it does today."

There's a lot going on in that last little bit. First, they paced with the customer's objection, and then they move them forward in time to picture a moment after they have purchased the CD player, and at that moment, they are feeling good.

When you are having a conversation, take note of the sensory modalities that are being used. Let's take a look at some examples:

- Visual – "short-sighted," "clear-cut," "sight for sore eyes," "paint a picture," "show me," "I see what you mean," "looks like a good idea"

- Auditory – "word for word," "rings a bell," "loud and clear," "I hear what you're saying"

- Kinesthetic – "get a handle on," "hot-headed," "get a load of this," "it just feels wrong"

You will discover that the more often you use the modalities that other people like, the easier your conversations will go.

Chapter 7: Declutter Your Mind and Kill Negativity

Everyone thinks that our minds were designed to hold a constant stream of thoughts, and there isn't anything you can do about it. Our minds are in charge, and we have to follow it. All the buzzing won't stop, and we are helpless to make it stop. This is so not true.

Our minds are a tool that we are able to control if we want to. It could be an asset that lets you experience all sorts of wonderful things. It could be a source of misery and pain if you allow it to fixate on negative thoughts like fear and everything it manifests.

The Mind's Cycle

A mind that hasn't been tamed love to feed you the same thoughts and generates the same exact experiences. A normal cycle goes something like this:

- Perception or interpretation

- Feelings and thoughts

- Beliefs

- Reaction

- Interaction

And it begins all over again. You might be wondering what is wrong with this cycle. There isn't anything wrong with it as long as you are feeling good and experiencing things that bring you joy.

If you are having reactions because of limiting beliefs and negative thoughts, you won't be able to control them, and you will be reacting negatively most of the time.

Our minds like to dwell on the negative instead of the positive.

49

Breaking the Cycle

In order to empty your mind, you have to let go of what is taking up precious space in your heart and mind that isn't serving you. It might look something like this:

- Interaction

- Perception

- Feelings and thoughts

- Empty mind

When you have processed everything that is on your mind, you will gain some perspective. You normally act when you need to, from truth and clarity. You aren't feeding the loop anymore.

When you have an empty mind, it will be:

- Energized: no effort will be wasted on any thoughts that aren't wanted

- Relaxed: it releases stress and will foster well being

- Creative: it lets new ideas and inspiration come in

- Free: no worries or judgment

- Intuitive: it receives input from higher sources

- Peaceful: it won't dwell on thoughts that are the same

- Aware: embraces the experience and moment

Ways to Empty Your Mind

You can do these anytime you need a break from the cycle of constant worrying and thinking.

1. Moving Your Body

Moving our bodies is a great way to release energy that has gotten stuck. You can do whatever you want as long as while you are doing it, you release what is on your mind.

If you like cardio, you could dance, ride a bike, run, or walk. If you like doing Pilates or yoga, go for it. The stretching and deep breathing will help ease the tension.

Hold a conversation with yourself while you exercise. You need to visualize all those unwanted feelings and thoughts, leaving as you exhale. This will give your self-esteem a boost. With regular exercise, you can release negativity while energizing your soul, body, and mind.

2. Writing

When my mind is full of buzzing, and I can't control the overloaded thoughts, this is my go-to choice. Writing is ranting on paper until you don't have anything else to say.

• What you Need

If you like writing it out using a pen and paper, don't go out and buy expensive stationery. Purchase a cheap notebook because you will be getting rid of it later.

If you are going to type it on your computer, disable spell check because you don't want to get distracted by all those squiggly lines.

• How You Do It

Begin writing about what you are feeling right now. Don't hold back anything. You can curse and swear or say whatever you want. This is your time, and you can say anything you would like.

Don't worry about grammar or spelling. You are with paper and a pen, and you can't take anything back. Continue until you don't have anything else to say. If you feel an insight and you think you have uncovered something, write down a word that represents this new idea a couple of times.

Never stop to highlight anything important. You are going to remember it if it is that important to you. Once you are finished, take a deep breath and tear or shred the paper. If you have been typing it out, just delete what you have typed.

- Challenges

Your mind is going to play tricks on you to make you justify and analyze. Just keep writing and remind yourself that you are dealing with it by writing it down, and you don't have to explain anything to anybody.

If you haven't written in a journal before, it might take you a bit longer than you thought it would. Just write for as long as possible. If you need to stop, keep an intention to finish it later. You will need to get back to it as quickly as possible. An intention is you making a promise to yourself. Never ignore it, or it will be added to your mental noise. Just like anything else, this will get easier with some practice.

- What Can You Expect

You are going to feel a lot lighter. You have just taken a huge load off of your mind. You might get an action or an insight about what you need to do. Be sure to write these down.

3. Meditation

This is the best way to calm an overactive mind. It is very simple, and you only need a few things for it: your willingness and stillness.

- How It's Done

You need to find a quiet place. It could be your care, office, or home. Set a timer for ten to 20 minutes. You probably shouldn't do more than 20 minutes if you are new to meditation.

Sit up straight either in a chair or on the floor, shut your eyes, and begin focusing on your breathing. Take some breaths and follow your breathing. Think of some things that you are thankful for and say them to yourself. Smile. While you smile, follow your breathing, breathe in and breathe out. Once the time is up, stop and then continue your day.

- Challenges

Your mind is going to resist at first, and you are going to get bored. Your brain will try to repeat the same thoughts to help feed the compulsion. Notice the thoughts as they come and then leave them alone. When you notice a thought, it will go on its way.

You are going to be tempted to check the time. If you have an urge to look, do it quickly but not again. If at all possible, tell yourself you have a timer set.

Your mind is going to wander, and you are going to lose focus on your breathing. This is all perfectly normal. Awareness will come in waves. Just try to ride it for as long as possible and catch the next one.

If you can't focus on your breath, begin counting every breath. If you lose count, start back at one. If you aren't a native English speaker, it might help if you count in your native language.

- Variations

If breathing is too hard, you could just repeat a mantra. Find one that resonates with you. Here are some examples to help you out:

  o   "I choose to trust. I let go."

  o   "I cherish myself; I cherish all beings."

- What You Can Expect

As stated above, you are going to have challenges; accept them. Smile as often and as much as possible. By the time you are done, you are going to feel at peace and calm. You will be able to handle your day and everything that happens. You will be open to new experiences and thoughts.

The more you get used to meditating; you will be able to explore all kinds of mantras and techniques. The things you say aren't as important as you what you are doing. If you are a beginner, keep it simple until you get into a routine.

NLP for Anxiety

Just about everybody will experience anxiety sometime in their lives. If you don't know how to handle it the right way, you might be putting your health at risk. In order to help you control your thoughts, you might benefit from learning some NLP techniques to help reduce your anxiety. NLP stands for Neuro-Linguistic Programming. This concept is fairly new, but it could help you fix your life the way you have always wanted it to be.

Every one of the NLP techniques is simple, and you just need to be willing to try. Knowing ways to handle anxiety the right way will help you reduce your stress levels and cope with everyday challenges. Life is too short not to be happy.

Let's look at how people experience anxiety and what NLP techniques you can try for yourself. These techniques aren't a magic potion for all your problems. Think of them as a way to understand yourself better and reprogramming your brain.

Here are some techniques you can use to control your anxiety:

Reframing

This is probably the most popular NLP technique used for anxiety. It is effective and simple since it can help you get rid of your negative thoughts and begin to make yourself look more on the brighter side of life.

- Using Reframing

You are basically going to change how you think about your anxiety. If you are totally honest with yourself, anxiety isn't a pleasant feeling. What would happen if you change that image and think of it as a blessing rather than a curse? The majority of the time, anxiety is trying to show you that you might need to listen more carefully to yourself and adjust what isn't helping you reach your goals.

- Practicing Reframing

    o   Never tell yourself things like: "I'm always anxious" or "I can't deal with the stress anymore." Rather, you can use phrases such as "I'm feeling a bit more challenged in my life right now, but it'll all work out for the best."

    o   Find and overcome the secondary part of the anxiety. This is the most important step of the entire process.

    Most of the time, you might be sabotaging yourself without even realizing it. You might be feeling stressed about your job, but you don't want to leave because you want others to feel sorry for you.

    You have to agree with your subconscious about what matters more. Do you want to feel at ease, or do you want others to feel sorry for you? You know the answer, don't you?

    o   Never let cortisol get the better of you. Notice what happens. When you experience anxiety, cortisol gets released, and your body screams PANIC! You have to learn not to let panic guide your life, choices, or decisions.

Anchoring

Anchoring could help you the most when going through a panic attack. This technique will pull you out of a panic state into a state of happiness and joy.

- Practicing Anchoring

Practice anchoring when you are calm and then use it when you start feeling anxious.

- o Use some meditation exercises to help you relax. Lie down and shut your eyes. Now, remember the happiest memory that you can. The more vividly you can make the image, the better it will help.

- o Allow positive emotions to fill your soul. Smile and relive the happy memory again. Feel this warmth going through your body.

- o Pick an anchor. The anchor could be anything that will bring you back to these positive feelings when you need to use them.

    Some people will do things like pinching themselves, pulling a finger, or pulling an earlobe. Each time you do this, you will experience these positive feelings that you associate with this happy memory.

Chapter 8: Maintaining Positivity

As humans, we are constantly faced with setbacks, difficulties, and challenges. We can't avoid these as they are an inevitable part of being human. When we learn how to manage our stress and respond with positive attitudes to every challenge, we will grow and begin moving forward in our lives.

If we don't have these setbacks, we can't learn what we need to know and develop our character qualities to what they are now. Most of our ability to succeed comes from how we manage stress and deal with our lives.

The best characteristics of superior women and men are they can recognize that temporary defeats and disappointments are inevitable, and they can accept them as being another part of their lives. They will do whatever they can to stay away from problems, but if problems arise, these superior people will respond with positive attitudes, learn what they can, and then move forward toward their dreams.

There will always be a tendency for us to emotionally react when we get frustrated. If things we hope for and want don't materialize, we are going to feel unhappy and disappointed. We will feel disillusioned and will react like we have been punched in the gut.

Keeping our positive attitudes is necessary if we are to achieve anything or if we want to improve our quality of life. There are many books that talk about how powerful positive thinking is. But this is a lot easier said than done.

Here are some ways to help you keep your positive attitude during whatever life might throw at you.

Figure Out Your Reality

It is important for you to figure out your reality by how you react to the world. If something happens, you are the only person who gets to choose whether it is a negative or positive experience and then react; however, you want. You might feel that losing your job is a disaster, or you could look at it as an opportunity for brighter and bigger things. YOU get to choose what it means to you.

Positive Attitudes While Managing Stress

A person who is optimistic knows how to handle stress in any situation and will soon move away from disappointment. They will respond fast to any adverse event and will see it as being external, specific, and temporary to themselves. An optimistic person will respond while keeping a positive attitude. They know ways to manage stress and counter these negative feelings by looking at the event so that it seems positive.

Our conscious mind is only able to hold onto one thought, whether it is negative or positive at one time. If you choose to keep positive thoughts, you will keep your emotions positive and your mind optimistic.

Because our feelings and thoughts determine our actions, we tend to be more constructive, and we will begin moving quickly forward toward the goals we've chosen.

Have a Strong Start to Your Day

Most people will drag their bodies out of bed, and this only creates a negative mind frame for the whole day. Positive people will create morning rituals that will reinforce how great their lives are and that they are happy to be alive.

I used to like waking up to Bon Jovi's "It's My Life" to get me up and going. Now, I begin my day listening or reading something positive. It doesn't matter if you have one minute, 20 minutes, or one hour to do your ritual, you get to begin your day; however, you would like.

Switch Your Language to Positive

This comes down to how you speak to yourself regularly. During our time of decision making and problem-solving, we need to change our language from being negative to being positive.

Here are three positive words to use to help you describe a hard time during your life:

1. Challenge

When you are having difficulties, you need to reframe it immediately. You need to choose to look at it as a challenge and then begin moving forward. Instead of stating, "I have a problem," say, "I have an interesting challenge facing me."

The word challenge is positive. It is things that you can rise to that will make you better and stronger. It's the same situation, but the word you use to describe it is different.

2. Situation

Rather than using the word problem, you need to use the situation. A problem is something you have to deal with. The situation is exactly the same, but it's the way you interpret this situation that makes it appear and sound totally different.

3. Opportunity

The best word to help you manage stress and keep your positive attitude is an opportunity.

If you are facing any type of difficulty, rather than saying: "I have a problem," you could say, "I am facing an unexpected opportunity."

If you can concentrate your powers on finding what the opportunity is, you will be able to find it. It might only be a lesson, but you will find it.

Exercise

Exercise has always been a good way to keep a positive attitude since the brain releases feel-good chemicals into the bloodstream while you exercise. Exercising is a great way to begin your day. You can exercise any way you would like. You can dance, do yoga, walking, running, swimming, just get out there and move your body.

Don't Let Problems Get You Down

You have to have the mindset that it doesn't matter what happens; you won't let it get you down. You will only respond with a positive and constructive attitude.

Take a deep breath to relax and find the good things about the situation you are facing. Never run away from the problem, accept, reflect and see the good to move on.

Fill Your Brain with Positivity

You can find millions of videos, podcasts, and books that you can use to inspire you to help you live the life you want. You could do this first thing in the morning or during your exercise routine while eating, cleaning, cooking, or even commuting... there will always be time for positivity.

Talk to Yourself Positively

You have to neutralize all negative emotions and thoughts by talking positively to yourself at all times. You can say things like, "I feel healthy! I feel happy! I feel terrific!"

While you are going about your day, say things like, "I like myself, and I love my work!"

The law of expression states that whatever gets expressed gets impressed. The things you say to others or yourself will get deeply impressed in your subconscious mind and will become a part of your personality permanently.

Be Around Positive People

It has been said many times that you will have the same level of lifestyle, income, and health as the five people you spend time with. If you want to be physically fit, then hang out with physically fit people. If you want to begin a new business, hang out with other business owners. If you would like to be more positive, be sure you are around positive people.

You Have To Face Difficulties in Order to Grow

It's impossible to grow, learn, and be successful without facing difficulties and adversity. You have to learn how to manage stress and push above the difficulties to become better. You need to welcome every difficulty by saying, "This is good." and look at the situation to see the good in it.

Appreciate Each Other

When you appreciate each other for doing something well, their smile, or their clothes, you will begin to create a chain reaction of positivity. Does it make you feel great when somebody compliments you? If you want to get more, you have to give them and watch what unfolds around you.

Move Toward Your Dreams and Goals

You have to constantly move forward by thinking about your dreams, goals, and the person you want to be. If things go temporarily wrong, just tell yourself, "I believe in the perfect outcome of every situation in my life."

You have to stay positive, cheerful, and resist the temptation to move toward disappointment and negativity. Look at disappointments as a way to get stronger. Look at it and yourself in an optimistic and positive way.

Keep moving towards your goals and becoming the best version of yourself.

What Goes in Comes Out the Same

You've heard the old expression: "Garbage In, Garbage Out." This expression comes from programming yourself to think that results will only be as good as what you put in. If you are feeding yourself on negativity all day, then you are going to feel negative, too.

There is a lot of media that thrives on negativity. You have to put yourself on a negativity diet. You will soon see how easy it is to keep a positive attitude.

Your Batteries Need Recharging

The main key to keeping your positive attitude is taking time to recharge your own batteries. This could mean taking a couple of hours each day to read a positive book or going on vacation.

If you aren't able to travel, you could take a staycation, where you just turn off the outside and spend time doing what you love.

Live Gratitude

There are so many positive things that happen during the day, and we usually ignore them. We constantly let negative comments ruin our moods. You could start a gratitude journal where you write down the things that you are grateful for throughout your day or each evening when you go to bed.

Stop Negative Thoughts

You can't be a positive person constantly, and you have to realize that negative thoughts will come up every now and then. These might be frequent, to begin with, but will lessen as you practice these tips. If you begin to notice a negative thought creeping up on you, you can use one of these tips to stop them.

The main idea is to interrupt your thought patterns and change your state of mind. I find it helpful when I sing the theme song to The Smurfs. If I begin to feel angry, sad, or frustrated, I just begin humming that song, and soon, I will have a big smile on my face.

You have several tips that will help you keep your positive attitude, but they aren't any use if you don't implement them in your life. Begin small. Choose the easiest one or one that speaks to you and introduce it into your life beginning this very moment. With time, begin implementing some other tips and watch your positivity get stronger.

Chapter 9: Self Esteem and Confidence

Having low self-esteem can have origins from traumatic childhood experiences like sexual, physical, or emotional abuse, neglect, or separation from parental figures. Later on, in life, your self-esteem could be undermined by a general sense of lack of control, frustrating or deficient relationships, getting divorced, or losing a job. Having a sense of no control might be seen in victims of discrimination based on sexual orientation, sex, race, culture, or religion, or victims of sexual, physical, or emotional abuse.

The relationship between mental distress, mental disorder, and low self-esteem is complex. Low self-esteem is a predisposition to mental disorders, which will then harm self-esteem. There are some cases where low self-esteem is the main feature of a mental disorder like borderline personality disorder or depression.

People who have low self-esteem see the world as being a hostile place with them being the victim. Because of this, they won't assert or express themselves. They will feel powerless to change things. They will miss out on opportunities and experiences. All of this will lower their self-esteem even more and thus pulling them down into an endless spiral.

On top of all this, we have to listen to the inner critic that is constantly telling us that we just aren't good enough. When we get bombarded by all these things that threaten our self-confidence, we have to take charge of building it back up.

If you think you are suffering from low self-esteem, there are some things you can do to give yourself a boost and break out of that spiral. You might be doing some of these, and you don't have to do all of them. Just do the ones that you feel comfortable with.

- Take on an Equality Mentality

People who have low self-esteem always see other people as more deserving or better than they are. Rather than thinking this way, you need to see yourself as equals. They aren't any more deserving or better than you. Make a mental turn to have an equal mentality, and you will see an improvement to your self-esteem.

- Create Boundaries

You have to learn to say no. You have to teach others to respect these boundaries. If you have to take a class about how to be assertive, learn to ask for the things you want. The more say and control you have over your life, the greater your self-esteem will be.

- Take Care of Yourself

Your self-esteem all depends on a combination of social health, emotional health, and physical health. It will be hard for you to feel good about yourself if you have low energy or you hate the way you look.

Pay attention to your hygiene. Trim your nails, brush your hair, take a shower, brush your teeth, etc.

Take some time to create good exercise routines, sleeping habits, and eating habits. Make mealtime special, even if you eat by yourself. Turn the television off, set the table, light some candles, and take time to be grateful. Try to walk daily, even when it is cold and rainy. Do exercises that make you sweat at least three times weekly.

You also have to dress how you feel. I know you have heard, "clothes make the man." Make sure you wear clothes that are clean and that make you feel good. Wearing clothes that are free from wrinkles will make you feel better than wearing an old crumpled t-shirt. Give your self-esteem a boost by taking the time to take care of your own needs.

- Think Positive

Tell yourself that in spite of all your problems, you are a valuable, special, and unique person. You have the right to feel good about yourself. You are a miracle of consciousness, the universe's consciousness. Find and challenge all negative thoughts you might have about yourself like "Nobody likes me," "I can't do anything right," or "I'm a loser."

- Create Two Lists

Make a list of your strengths and another one for your achievements. Get a relative or friend that is supportive to help you with the lists. People who have low self-esteem aren't normally in the best mind frame. Once you have the lists made, keep them in a safe place. Read them each day.

- Help Others

When you help somebody else, it allows you to forget about yourself and to be grateful for everything you have. It makes you feel good when you can make a difference in somebody else's life.

Rather than focusing on your weaknesses, you could teach someone else, volunteer to mentor teens, or assist others. You will soon see your self-confidence begin to grow.

- Set Goals You Can Achieve

There are too many people who get discouraged about what they are able to do because they will set goals that they just can't reach. Begin by creating small goals that you can reach easily.

When you have created a successful stream that makes you feel great, you can move to goals that are a bit harder. Be sure you keep a list of your achievements, whether they are small or large, to keep yourself reminded about the things that you have done and done well.

Rather than focusing on all your "to-dos," take some time to reflect on your "did-it" list. When you look back on all your goals, projects, and milestone that you have reached, you will be able to reinforce your confidence skills.

- Rejection Challenge

Jia Jiang became famous for his "busting fear" experience. He made a crazy request of people just so they would reject him for 100 days. The purpose of this experiment was to desensitize the rejection process after he got upset from being rejected by an investor. Getting rid of fear isn't easy. If you would like to have fun while building your self-confidence, this is a great way to do it.

- Clean Living Space

You need to make your living space attractive, comfortable, and clean. You will be surprised at how great you will feel just by watering your plants. Put items out that remind you of special people, times, and achievements.

- Inner Critic

The harshest comments that we get usually come from our inner critic. If you have problems with low self-confidence, it is possible that your inner critic is overactive and very inaccurate.

You can use cognitive behavioral therapy to help you begin questioning this inner critic. Find evidence that denies or supports all the things your inner critic is telling you. If you think you have failed, you can ask, "What evidence is there to support the thought that I am a failure?" and "What evidence is there that doesn't support the thought that I am a failure?"

Take all the opportunities you can to congratulate, reward, and compliment yourself, even for the tiniest of successes.

- Do What You Enjoy

You have every right to spoil yourself every now and then. You need to do one thing each day that you enjoy doing.

- Do What Scares You

The best for you to overcome your fears is to face them head-on. When you do things that scare you each day, you will be gaining confidence from each of these experiences. You will see your self-confidence begin to soar. Face your fears and get out of the comfort zone. You have to do one thing that scares you daily.

- Be Artistic

Dancing, poetry, music, and painting can reduce stress levels, interact positively with others, and lets you express yourself. You may even impress yourself by doing things you didn't think you could do. You could find a class at your community center or local adult education services.

- Affirm Yourself

You normally behave the way you think you should. The big trick to creating lasting changes is to change the way you look at yourself.

Affirmations are uplifting and positive statements that you can say to yourself. These are very effective when you say them out loud, so you hear yourself say it. You have a tendency to believe everything we tell ourselves all the time. If you don't like your appearance, say things that you like about yourself when you look in the mirror.

In order to get your brain to accept these things faster, put these affirmations as questions like, "Why am I so good at making deals?" rather than "I am very good at making deals." The brain is biologically wired to look for answers without analyzing the question's validity.

- Do Things you've Been Putting Off

We all hate making our to-do lists, but if we can accomplish just one of those, we will soon have the entire list done. Do things like weeding the garden, painting the kitchen, and putting away the paperwork.

- Imagine You the Way You Want You

Visualization is a technique where we see an image of whatever. You need to visualize an image of yourself that makes you proud. If you struggle with low self-confidence, you will have an inaccurate perception of yourself. Practice imagining this version of yourself, reaching all your goals.

- Be Nice to Others

You need to be nice and do nice things for others. You could talk to the postman, cashier, visit a sick friend, volunteer at a charity, or invite your new neighbor over for tea. When you put a smile on somebody's face, it will put one on yours, too.

- Stay Away from Places and People that Make You Feel Bad

This might mean you need to be more assertive. If you have problems being assertive, ask your doctor about assertiveness training.

- Spend Time with People You Love

While spending time with these people, try enlarging our social circle by meeting new friends.

- Ask for Support

Let your relatives and friends know what you are going through and ask for support and advice. They might be having similar problems, and you might be able to work together and create a support group. Never be too reserved or shy because most people like helping others.

- Create a Challenge you can Do

Throw a dinner party, learn to sing, take a painting class, or take up yoga; just do something fun and creative for your friends.

Remember the wise words from Lao Tzu, "Health is the greatest possession. Contentment is the greatest treasure. Confidence is the greatest friend.

Chapter 10: 16 Other Things to Make You Happy

Everybody wants to be healthy and happy. There are many things that you can do that can make a huge impact on your well being. It could be something as simple as reading your favorite book, keeping a journal, or looking at the stars. The bad news is we have to constantly work at being happy. Here are some things that researchers have found that can lift your spirits and help keep them high.

Find a Skill to Master

Working to improve an ability or skill like solving a difficult math problem or learning how to drive might increase your stress levels for a little while but will make you feel happy in the long run.

People tend to give up on a goal because it is stressful and hard to do. There is a benefit of learning how to do something well. You don't even have to reach your goal to feel happy and help your wellbeing.

Exercise

Working out has been proven to increase the release of dopamine in the brain. This is a chemical that can help relieve anxiety and depression and reduce stress.

You can easily reach these changes in only 20 minutes of exercise. The good news is that these benefits will last for 12 hours after your workout is over. It has been proven that people who are active are more satisfied and happier in their lives.

The location and how long your workout will affect your level of happiness after your workout is over.

Have Lunch Outside

If you constantly eat lunch at your desk or inside, it can have an adverse effect on your mood. One study measured how happy employees were after they had lunch in various locations.

These results showed the happiest workers at lunch at a beach, and the ones who were least happy ate at their desks or indoors. Being out in the sun helps stave off misery. Eating in the park or out in the sun will give your attitude a boost.

Put Your Hands in the Dirt

One study has found that bacteria that are common in the soil can produce the same effects as some antidepressant drugs. The smell of dirt could lift your spirits. A harmless bacteria called Mycobacterium vaccae can stimulate serotonin to be released in the brain. Having a low level of serotonin is why many people are depressed.

Cancer patients reported an increased quality of life after they were injected with the bacteria. These findings make us wonder if we shouldn't spend all day playing in the dirt.

Be Realistic and Optimistic

People that have a realists' rational outlook paired with an optimists' positive attitude are usually happier and more successful. This is because these "realistic optimists" have a perfect personality blend that helps them succeed. They are different from idealists because they are willing to face situations that are challenging, along with having a clear view of reality. They will use their positive outlook and creativity to work out their problems.

Have Sex

If you can remember, there was a study done back in 2004 that said if you increased the amount of sex you had from one time a month to weekly, it would make you as happy as getting $50,000.

But be careful. Having more sex doesn't mean more happiness. The researchers of the study released a report that the couples who had sex for the study reported that the sex they had wasn't enjoyable, and it didn't make them any happier.

This means that sex only leads to happiness if the couple is having sex for good reasons. It doesn't matter if it is once a month or once a week, the frequency isn't as important as the reasons behind it.

Never Hold Grudges

It is perfectly fine to get upset when someone has done something wrong to you. But it is completely different to hold onto that emotion for a long time. This is called "holding a grudge," and it could consume you if you aren't very careful.

The main reason this is bad for you is due to the negative emotions that are associated with grudges will create a way for resentment and could cause you to begin thinking about getting revenge. This won't leave any room in your emotional reserves for anything such as happiness to live. Research has linked this act to have better heart health, a longer life, improved physical abilities, and less stress.

This is why it will always be better to forgive and move forward than to hold on to grudges.

Smile

It may not surprise you that smiling will make you feel better. The important thing to remember here is the smile has to be real. It can't be a fake one. If you fake a smile, you could make yourself even more unhappy.

One study examined some bus drivers for two weeks. They saw employees who pasted a fake smile on their faces were in a worse mood at the end of their shift as compared to when they began their shift. The drivers who truly smiled because of positive thoughts had a much better mood at the end of their shift. When you smile, you have to make sure that you mean it.

Spend Time with Friends

Spending time with friends could make you happier than spending time with your family. In one study, researchers used the Mappiness app to find out if people would be happier if they were with their children, parents, or friends.

The app would send alerts, asking them how they felt. They had to choose either "extremely" or "not at all" during their day. Researchers analyzed over three million submissions and found that people would experience an average of an eight percent happiness increase while spending time with friends. There was only a 0.7 percent increase while spending time with children and 1.4 percent with parents.

Volunteer

This may sound counterintuitive to you, but a good way you can care for yourself is by taking care of others. In one study, researchers found that volunteering was more important than any other to boost their psychological health. Many volunteers have stated they had a reduced risk of death from a physical illness, higher satisfaction, and reduced risk of depression.

Buy Things for Others

If you have had a completely horrible day, you may have an urge to go out and purchase your favorite food or get that cute pair of shoes you've had your eye on for several months now. But research has proven that you will be happier if you take that money and spend it on somebody else rather than yourself.

One study done in 2008 gave some volunteers an envelope of money. Some volunteers were told to spend the money on others, and some were told they could spend it on themselves. The participants were asked to record their level of happiness before they got the money and then after they have spent the money at the end of the same day.

The researchers found that the participants who spent the money on others were happier than the ones who spent it on themselves.

Put Your Feelings on Paper

Have you ever had someone tell you: "If you are angry at somebody, write them a letter but don't send it." This may seem like a total waste of time, but science has revealed that writing your feelings down will help clarify your thoughts, relieve stress, and help you solve your problems better.

Some psychologists have found a neurological reason behind why this actually helps overcome emotional distress. These psychologists studied the brain scans of volunteers who had written down their emotional experiences for 20 minutes a day for four days. They compared these scans with volunteers who wrote down an inconsequential experience for the same time frame. The scans for the first group showed activity in the brain that is responsible for lessening emotional feelings. This suggests that writing down our experiences can help calm them in our minds. This activity wasn't present in the participants who wrote down an inconsequential experience.

Set a Specific Goal that You Can Reach

If you like making lists, you need to listen. When you set your goals, it would be best if you could set goals that are specific, so you know you will be able to achieve it. Rather than saying, "save the planet," say "recycle more."

The above examples were tested on 127 participants. The first group was given a goal of "increasing recycling," and the other group was given the goal of "saving the environment." The second group finished their task, but they didn't feel as satisfied with themselves as the first group did. The participants in the second group had lower personal happiness after they completed their goal.

Take a Nature Walk

If you live in the city and you are feeling down, I have good news, taking a brief walk in nature might be what it takes to get rid of those negative vibes.

We split 38 people into two groups. One group took an hour and a half minute walk in nature while the other group walked in the city. The people who walked in nature said they had less negative thoughts about themselves after their walk than they did before the walk. The people who walked in the city did not report a change at all.

Their fMRI brain scans showed less activity in the sgPFC or subgenual prefrontal cortex. This is the region of the brain that plays a key role in certain mood disorders. These have been linked with negative thought patterns. The people who walked in the city didn't show these benefits.

Meditate

There are many studies that show meditating can lessen feelings of anxiety and depression. Meditating is just being quiet and focusing on the present moments. Some research done with Buddhist monks shows that their brains have an area that is well developed that might be linked to emotional control and heightened awareness. It is possible that these people will be able to meditate better. There are studies that show people who have completed a meditation program show changes in the brain that are linked to memory, perspective, and self-awareness.

Drink Coffee

It isn't called "central perk" for nothing. It is a stimulant for the central nervous system. Caffeine boosts more than alertness; it could improve your mood.

Many studies have found a connection between drinking caffeine and the lesser risk of depression and a lower risk of suicide. One study found a connection with coffee and not tea. Other studies found the same effects for tea.

Conclusion

Thank you for making it through to the end of *Emotional Intelligence through NLP*. Let's hope it was informative and able to provide you with all of the tools you need to achieve your goals, whatever they may be.

The next step is to choose what area of your life you want to start making changes to. This could either be very obvious to you, or it could take some thinking to figure out. Whatever you decide on changing first, pick an NLP strategy that you believe will work well for you and your goal. You have the power in you to create a life that you have always wanted and deserve. NLP can help you to do just that. You have the techniques laid out before you, so now, it's up to you to use it to improve your life.

Finally, if you found this book useful in any way, a review on Amazon is always appreciated!